Last Thing at Night

Last Thing at Night

Prayers and readings
for the end of the day

Compiled by Rima Devereaux

DARTON·LONGMAN+TODD

First published in 2011 by
Darton, Longman and Todd Ltd
1 Spencer Court
140–142 Wandsworth High Street
London SW18 4JJ

ISBN 978-0-232-52884-8

A catalogue record for this book is available from the British
Library.

Designed and produced by Judy Linard
Printed and bound in Great Britain by Page Bros, Norwich, Norfolk

Contents

Introduction   7

Week One   9

Week Two   25

Week Three   45

Week Four   65

Week Five   83

Week Six   101

Sources and Acknowledgements   121

Further Reading   125

Introductory and Concluding Prayers   126

To Rob

Introduction

At the beginning of John's Gospel, two of John the Baptist's disciples follow Jesus and ask him where he lives. He invites them to come and see and they stay with him. They may have spent the evening with him.[*] Through the reflections in this book, Jesus invites us to do the same, to come and spend each evening with him and prepare with him for the night's rest.

This book is a collection of prayers and readings for use 'last thing at night', before going to bed. The end of the day is a time for taking stock of the day's events, surrendering them to God, and preparing for sleep, as well as for meditating on the darkness of the world and how the light of Christ comes to fill it and dwell within it. The readings I have chosen follow these twin themes of literal and metaphorical night.

Preparing this book has been a wonderful journey of discovering the richness of the Church's tradition and the abundance of Bible verses appropriate to the theme of the end of the day. I am hoping that you too, as reader, will enjoy coming with me on this journey of reflective surrender. It is my hope that the book will become an inspirational companion to keep by the bedside.

The book is also an invitation to the reader to follow the monastic tradition of marking the day with prayers

---

[*] This passage is quoted on Saturday of Week 2 below.

and readings. It is loosely based around the Church's Night Prayer (Compline), a prayer traditionally said last thing at night. Many of the readings are taken from the works of the Carmelite saints, because the Carmelite tradition is particularly rich in evocations of the metaphorical night and the need for surrender to God.

I have supplied enough material for 42 days altogether, arranged in six week-long sections. For each day there is an opening psalm, a Gospel reading and a reading from the Church's tradition. The introductory and concluding prayers are always the same, and you will soon come to memorise them. They are printed at the back of the book: a standard prayer to start, and at the end, after the reading of the day, the Nunc Dimittis, a blessing and the Salve Regina.

I suggest you take time to ponder each phrase, savouring the passage until it speaks to you (following the ancient monastic tradition of *lectio divina*). You might want to put the book down at any moment and let reading give way to silent prayer. Feel free to sit loose to the structure given here, and to use it as a springboard for your own personal end-of-day communion with God.

I would like to thank Brendan Walsh, my editor at Darton, Longman and Todd, for approaching me with the original idea for this book, and for his unfailing good humour and patience with the foibles of a first-time author; thanks also go to the editorial and production teams. I also wish to thank Joanne Moseley and Austen Ivereigh who kindly supplied their favourite readings for inclusion in the book.

Week One

Introductory prayer

Psalm 4
When I call, answer me, God, upholder of my right,
In my distress you have set me at large;
take pity on me and hear my prayer!

Children of men, how long will you be heavy of
   heart,
why love what is vain and chase after illusions?

Realise that Yahweh performs wonders for his
   faithful,
Yahweh listens when I call to him.

Be careful not to sin,
speak in your hearts, and on your beds keep silence.

Loyally offer sacrifices, and trust in Yahweh.

Many keep saying, 'Who will put happiness before our
   eyes?'
Let the light of your face shine on us.

Yahweh, to my heart you are a richer joy
than all their corn and new wine.

In peace I lie down and at once fall asleep,
for it is you and none other, Yahweh, who make me rest
    secure.

Gospel reading: Luke 17.7–10

'Which of you, with a servant ploughing or minding
sheep, would say to him when he returned from the
fields, "Come and have your meal at once"? Would he
not be more likely to say, "Get my supper ready; fasten
your belt and wait on me while I eat and drink. You
yourself can eat and drink afterwards"? Must he be
grateful to the servant for doing what he was told? So
with you: when you have done all you have been told to
do, say, "We are useless servants: we have done no more
than our duty."'

Reading from the Church's tradition

And when night comes, and retrospect shows that
everything was patchwork and much which one had
planned left undone, when so many things rouse shame
and regret, then take all as it is, lay it in God's hands, and
offer it up to Him. In this way we will be able to rest in Him,
actually to rest, and to begin the new day like a new life.

Edith Stein, *Essays on Woman*, p. 145

Concluding prayers

TUESDAY

Introductory prayer

Psalm 6

Yahweh, let your rebuke to me not be in
    anger,
your punishment not in the heat of wrath.
Have pity on me, Yahweh, for I am fading away.
Heal me, Yahweh, my bones are shaken,
my spirit is shaken to its very depths.
But you, Yahweh . . . how long?

Yahweh, relent and save my life
rescue me because of your faithful love,
for in death there is no remembrance of you;
who could sing your praises in Sheol?

I am worn out with groaning,
every night I drench my pillow
and soak my bed with tears.
My eyes waste away with vexation.
Arrogance from all my foes!
Away from me, all evil-doers!

For Yahweh has heard the sound of my
    weeping,
Yahweh has heard my pleading.
Yahweh will accept my prayer.

Let all my enemies be put to confusion, shaken to their
    depths,
let them retreat in sudden confusion.

Gospel reading: Mark 1.32-34

That evening, after sunset, they brought to him all who
were sick and those who were possessed by devils. The
whole town came crowding round the door, and he
cured many who were sick with diseases of one kind
or another; he also drove out many devils, but he would
not allow them to speak, because they knew who he
was.

Reading from the Church's tradition

This is a simple exercise which can be done towards
the end of each day. First, recall those moments of the
day which you have enjoyed, relish them and thank
God for them. These moments are God's gift, signs of
God's self-giving to you.

Then pray for enlightenment, so that you can
recognise God at work in you. Look first at your moods
and feelings during the day, but without any judging or
moralising. Then ask yourself, 'What were the desires
underlying my moods? Was it desire for my personal
kingdom of wealth, status etc., or was it desire for God's
Kingdom of truth, justice, peace and compassion?'

Gerard W. Hughes, *God of Compassion*, p. 76

Concluding prayers

WEDNESDAY

Introductory prayer

Psalm 8

Yahweh our Lord,
how majestic is your name throughout the world!

Whoever keeps singing of your majesty higher than the
    heavens,
even through the mouths of children, or of babes in
    arms,
you make him a fortress, firm against your foes,
to subdue the enemy and the rebel.

I look up at your heavens, shaped by your fingers,
at the moon and the stars you set firm –
what are human beings that you spare a thought for
    them,
or the child of Adam that you care for him?

Yet you have made him little less than a god,
you have crowned him with glory and beauty,
made him lord of the works of your hands,
put all things under his feet,

sheep and cattle, all of them,
and even the wild beasts,
birds in the sky, fish in the sea,
when he makes his way across the ocean.

Yahweh our Lord,
how majestic your name throughout the world!

Gospel reading: Matthew 7.7-11

'Ask, and it will be given to you; search, and you will find; knock, and the door will be opened to you. Everyone who asks receives; everyone who searches finds; everyone who knocks will have the door opened. Is there anyone among you who would hand is son a stone when he asked for bread? Or would hand him a snake when he asked for a fish? If you, then, evil as you are, know how to give your children what is good, how much more will your Father in heaven give good things to those who ask him!'

Reading from the Church's tradition

Abandonment . . . that is what allows us to surrender to God. I am quite young, but it seems to me that I have really suffered at times. Oh, then, when everything was dark, when the present was so painful and the future seemed even more gloomy to me, I used to close my eyes and abandon myself like a child in the arms of this Father who is in Heaven.

Elizabeth of the Trinity, *Letters from Carmel*, Letter 129, p. 57

Concluding prayers

THURSDAY

Introductory prayer

Psalm 11
In Yahweh I have found refuge.
How can you say to me,
'Bird, flee to your mountain?

'For look, the wicked are drawing their bows,
fitting their arrows to the string
to shoot honest men from the shadows.
If the foundations fall to ruin, what can the upright do?'

Yahweh in his holy temple!
Yahweh, his throne is in heaven;
his eyes watch over the world,
his gaze scrutinises the children of Adam.

Yahweh examines the upright and the wicked,
the lover of violence he detests.
He will rain down red-hot coals,
fire and sulphur on the wicked,
a scorching wind will be their lot.

For Yahweh is upright and loves uprightness,
the honest will ever see his face.

Gospel reading: John 3.19-21

'And the judgement is this:
though the light has come into the world
people have preferred darkness to the light
because their deeds were evil.
And indeed, everybody who does wrong
hates the light and avoids it,
to prevent his actions from being shown up;
but whoever does the truth
comes out into the light,
so that what he is doing may plainly appear as done in
    God.'

Reading from the Church's tradition

Welcome one another, says the apostle, as Christ
welcomed us, for the glory of God. A divided household
cannot last and only a united community is capable of
giving hospitality.

Each day and every instant of the day open your
inmost heart to your brothers and sisters. Love them just
as they are, not as you would wish them to be. What is the
use of endless outside contacts, if at home there is no real
acceptance of one another? Be humble always, gentle and
patient. Be forbearing with one another and charitable.
Open-heartedness in community will teach you how far
you may open your doors to the outside world.

In the Heart of the City, In the Heart of God, p. 33

Concluding prayers

FRIDAY

Introductory prayer

Psalm 13

How long, Yahweh, will you forget me? For ever?
How long will you turn away your face from me?
How long must I nurse rebellion in my soul,
sorrow in my heart day and night?
How long is the enemy to domineer over me?
Look down, answer me, Yahweh my God!
Give light to my eyes or I shall fall into the sleep of
    death.

Or my foe will boast, 'I have overpowered him,'
and my enemy have the joy of seeing me stumble.
As for me, I trust in your faithful love, Yahweh.
Let my heart delight in your saving help,
let me sing to Yahweh for his generosity to me,
let me sing to the name of Yahweh the Most High!

Gospel reading: Mark 10.17-22

He was setting out on a journey when a man ran up,
knelt before him and put this question to him, 'Good
master, what must I do to inherit eternal life?' Jesus said
to him, 'Why do you call me good? No one is good but
God alone. You know the commandments: *You shall not
kill; You shall not commit adultery; You shall not steal;
You shall not give false witness; You shall not defraud;*

Honour your father and mother.' And he said to him, 'Master, I have kept all these since my earliest days.' Jesus looked steadily at him and he was filled with love for him, and he said, 'You need to do one thing more. Go and sell what you own and give the money to the poor, and you will have treasure in heaven; then come, follow me.' But his face fell at these words and he went away sad, for he was a man of great wealth.

Reading from the Church's tradition

For I know well the spring that flows and runs,
although it is night.
1. That eternal spring is hidden,
for I know well where it has its rise,
although it is night . . .
3. I know that nothing else is so beautiful,
and that the heavens and the earth drink there,
although it is night . . .
5. Its clarity is never darkened,
and I know that every light has come from it,
although it is night.

John of the Cross, 'Song of the soul that rejoices in
knowing God through faith', pp. 58–9

Concluding prayers

SATURDAY

Introductory prayer

Psalm 16
Protect me, O God, in you is my refuge.

To Yahweh I say, 'You are my Lord,
my happiness is in none of the sacred spirits of the
    earth.'

They only take advantage of all who love them.
People flock to their teeming idols.
Never shall I pour libations to them!
Never take their names on my lips.

My birthright, my cup is Yahweh;
you, you alone, hold my lot secure.
The measuring-line marks out for me a delightful place,
my birthright is all I could wish.

I bless Yahweh who is my counsellor,
even at night my heart instructs me.
I keep Yahweh before me always,
for with him at my right hand, nothing can shake me.

So my heart rejoices, my soul delights,
my body too will rest secure,
for you will not abandon me to Sheol,

you cannot allow your faithful servant to see the abyss.
You will teach me the path of life,
unbounded joy in your presence,
at your right hand delight for ever.

Gospel reading: John 20.19–23

In the evening of that same day, the first day of the week, the doors were closed in the room where the disciples were, for fear of the Jews. Jesus came and stood among them. He said to them, 'Peace be with you,' and, after saying this, he showed them his hands and his side. The disciples were filled with joy at seeing the Lord, and he said to them again, 'Peace be with you.

'As the Father sent me,
so am I sending you.'

After saying this he breathed on them and said:

Receive the Holy Spirit.
If you forgive anyone's sins,
they are forgiven;
if you retain anyone's sins,
they are retained.

Reading from the Church's tradition

In this contemplation, as I have already written, we don't do anything ourselves. Neither do we labor, nor do we bargain, nor is anything else necessary –

because everything else is an impediment and hindrance – than to say *fiat voluntas tua:* Your will, Lord, be done in me in every way and manner that You, my Lord, want. If You want it to be done with trials, strengthen me and let them come; if with persecutions, illnesses, dishonors, and a lack of life's necessities, here I am; I will not turn away, my Father, nor is it right that I turn my back on You. Since Your Son gave You this will of mine in the name of all, there's no reason for any lack on my part. But grant me the favor of Your kingdom that I may do Your will, since He asked for this kingdom for me, and use me as You would Your own possession, in conformity with Your will.

Teresa of Avila, *The Way of Perfection*,
ch. 32, para. 10, pp. 163–4

Concluding prayers

SUNDAY

Introductory prayer

Psalm 18, vv. 28–34

Yahweh, you yourself are my lamp,
my God lights up my darkness;
with you I storm the rampart,
with my God I can scale any wall.

This God, his way is blameless;
the word of Yahweh is refined in the furnace,
for he alone is the shield
of all who take refuge in him.

For who is God but Yahweh,
who is a rock but our God?
This God who girds me with strength
who makes my way free from blame,

who makes me as swift as a deer
and sets me firmly on the heights,
who trains my hands for battle,
my arms to bend a bow of bronze.

Gospel reading: Luke 6.12–16

Now it happened in those days that he went onto the
mountain to pray; and he spent the whole night in prayer
to God. When day came he summoned his disciples and

picked out twelve of them; he called them 'apostles': Simon whom he called Peter, and his brother Andrew, James, John, Philip, Bartholomew, Matthew, Thomas, James son of Alphaeus, Simon called the Zealot, Judas son of James, and Judas Iscariot who became a traitor.

Reading from the Church's tradition

Just as a torrent, throwing itself with impetuosity into the ocean, drags after it everything it encounters in its passage, in the same way, O Jesus, the soul who plunges into the shoreless ocean of Your Love, draws with her all the treasures she possesses. Lord, You know it, I have no other treasures than the souls it has pleased You to unite to mine; it is You who entrusted these treasures to me, and so I dare to borrow the words You addressed to the heavenly Father, the last night which saw You on our earth as a traveler and a mortal. Jesus, I do not know when my exile will be ended; more than one night will still see me singing Your Mercies in his exile, but for me will finally come *the last night*, and then I want to be able to say to You, O my God:

'I have glorified you on earth; I have finished the work you gave me to do. And now do you, Father, glorify me with yourself, with the glory I had with you before the world existed.'

Thérèse of Lisieux, *Story of a Soul*, pp. 254–5

Concluding prayers

Week Two

MONDAY

Introductory prayer

Psalm 23
Yahweh is my shepherd, I lack nothing.
In grassy meadows he lets me lie.

By tranquil streams he leads me
to restore my spirit.
He guides me in paths of saving justice
as befits his name.

Even were I to walk in a ravine as dark as death
I should fear no danger, for you are at my side.
Your staff and your crook are there to soothe me.

You prepare a table for me
under the eyes of my enemies;
you anoint my head with oil;
my cup brims over.

Kindness and faithful love pursue me
every day of my life.

I make my home in the house of Yahweh
for all time to come.

Gospel reading: Matthew 6.25, 31–34

'That is why I am telling you not to worry about your life and what you are to eat, nor about your body and what you are to wear. Surely life is more than food, and the body more than clothing! . . . So do not worry; do not say: "What are we to eat? What are we to drink? What are we to wear?" It is the gentiles who set their hearts on all these things. Your heavenly Father knows you need them all. Set your hearts on his kingdom first, and on God's saving justice, and all these other things will be given you as well. So do not worry about tomorrow: tomorrow will take care of itself. Each day has enough trouble of its own.'

Reading from the Church's tradition

Pray *in the evening*, with those coming back from work, as night draws on, at the beginning of each watch and turn everything into thanksgiving – Eucharist. . . . Every week, on Thursdays, remember Gethsemane, where there was no one to pray for an hour with Jesus, and *pray in the night* in the midst of the joys and miseries of the city, where God has placed you like watchmen watching for the dawn. Beg forgiveness for your own sins and thank God for his marvels; rise in the middle of the night to thank him for his just judgements. The Church has called us to be the watchmen to alert the people, and to be awake on the city ramparts. You too, get up in the night at the beginning of each watch to pour out your heart like water before the Lord your God.

In the Heart of the City, In the Heart of God,
pp. 17–18

Concluding prayers

TUESDAY

Introductory prayer

Psalm 27, vv. 1-5

Yahweh is my light and my salvation,
whom should I fear?
Yahweh is the fortress of my life,
whom should I dread?

When the wicked advance against me
to eat me up,
they, my opponents, my enemies,
are the ones who stumble and fall.

Though an army pitch camp against me,
my heart will not fear,
though war break out against me,
my trust will never be shaken.

One thing I ask of Yahweh,
one thing I seek:
to dwell in Yahweh's house
all the days of my life,
to enjoy the sweetness of Yahweh,
to seek out his temple.

For he hides me away under his roof
on the day of evil,

he folds me in the recesses of his tent,
sets me high on a rock.

Gospel reading: Mark 4.35−41
With the coming of evening that same day, he said to
them, 'Let us cross over to the other side.' And leaving
the crowd behind they took him, just as he was, in the
boat; and there were other boats with him. Then it
began to blow a great gale and the waves were
breaking into the boat so that it was almost swamped.
But he was in the stern, his head on the cushion,
asleep. They woke him and said to him, 'Master, do you
not care? We are lost!' And he woke up and rebuked the
wind and said to the sea, 'Quiet now! Be calm!' And the
wind dropped, and there followed a great calm. Then
he said to them, 'Why are you so frightened? Have you
still no faith?' They were overcome with awe and said
to one another, 'Who can this be? Even the wind and
the sea obey him.'

Reading from the Church's tradition
We surrender to the attraction of interior silence,
tranquillity, and peace. We do not try to feel anything,
reflect about anything. Without effort, without trying,
we sink into this Presence, letting everything else go.
Let love alone speak: the simple desire to be one with
the Presence, to forget self, and to rest in the Ultimate
Mystery. This Presence is immense, yet so humble;
awe-inspiring, yet so gentle; limitless, yet so intimate,

tender and personal. I *know* that I am *known*. . . . We wait patiently; in silence, openness, and quiet attentiveness; motionless within and without. We surrender to the attraction to be still, to be loved, just to *be*.

Thomas Keating, *Open Mind, Open Heart*, p. 137

Concluding prayers

WEDNESDAY

Introductory prayer

Psalm 31, vv. 1-7

In you, Yahweh, I have taken refuge,
let me never be put to shame,
in your saving justice deliver me, rescue me,
turn your ear to me, make haste.

Be for me a rock-fastness,
a fortified citadel to save me.
You are my rock, my rampart;
true to your name, lead me and guide me!

Draw me out of the net they have spread for me,
for you are my refuge;
to your hands I commit my spirit,
by you have I been redeemed.

God of truth, you hate
those who serve useless idols;
but my trust is in Yahweh:
I will delight and rejoice in your faithful love!

Gospel reading: John 8.12

When Jesus spoke to the people again, he said:
I am the light of the world;
anyone who follows me

will not be walking in the dark,
but will have the light of life.

Reading from the Church's tradition
My Beloved, the mountains,
and lonely wooded valleys,
strange islands,
and resounding rivers,
the whistling of love-stirring breezes,

the tranquil night
at the time of the rising dawn,
silent music,
sounding solitude,
the supper that refreshes, and deepens love.

John of the Cross, 'The spiritual canticle',
stanzas 13 and 14, p. 46

Concluding prayers

THURSDAY

Introductory prayer

Psalm 32, vv. 1–7

How blessed are those whose offence is forgiven,
whose sin blotted out.
How blessed are those to whom Yahweh imputes no
    guilt,
whose spirit harbours no deceit.

I said not a word, but my bones wasted away
from groaning all the day;
day and night
your hand lay heavy upon me;
my heart grew parched as stubble
in summer drought.

I made my sin known to you,
did not conceal my guilt.
I said, 'I shall confess
my offence to Yahweh.'
And you, for your part, took away my guilt,
forgave my sin.

That is why each of your faithful ones prays to you
in time of distress.
Even if great floods overflow,
they will never reach your faithful.

You are a refuge for me,
you guard me in trouble,
with songs of deliverance you surround me.

Gospel reading: Matthew 11.28–30

'Come to me, all you who labour and are overburdened, and I will give you rest. Shoulder my yoke and learn from me, for I am gentle and humble in heart, *and you will find rest for your souls*. Yes, my yoke is easy and my burden light.'

Reading from the Church's tradition

We seem to think that everything is done when we willingly take and wear the religious habit and abandon all wordly things and possessions for Him. . . . There is no doubt that if a person perseveres in this nakedness and detachment from all worldly things he will reach his goal. But this perseverance includes the condition – and note that I am advising you of this – that you consider yourselves useless servants, as St. Paul, or Christ, says; and believe that you have not put our Lord under any obligation to grant you these kinds of favors. Rather, as one who has received more, you are more indebted. What can we do for a God so generous that He died for us, created us, and gives us being? Shouldn't we consider ourselves lucky to be able to repay something of what we owe Him for His service toward us? I say these words 'His service toward us' unwillingly; but the fact is that He did nothing else but

serve us all the time he lived in this world. And yet we
ask Him again for favors and gifts.

Teresa of Avila, *The Interior Castle*, 3.1.8, p. 308

Concluding prayers

FRIDAY

Introductory prayer

Psalm 36, vv. 5-12

Yahweh, your faithful love is in the heavens,
your constancy reaches to the clouds,
your saving justice is like towering mountains,
your judgements like the mighty deep.

Yahweh, you support both man and beast;
how precious, God, is your faithful love.
So the children of Adam
take refuge in the shadow of your wings.

They feast on the bounty of your house,
you let them drink from your delicious streams;
in you is the source of life,
by your light we see the light.

Maintain your faithful love to those who acknowledge
    you,
and your saving justice to the honest of heart.
Do not let the foot of the arrogant overtake me
or wicked hands drive me away.

There they have fallen, the evil-doers,
flung down, never to rise again.

Gospel reading: Luke 22.39-46

He then left to make his way as usual to the Mount of Olives, with the disciples following. When he reached the place he said to them, 'Pray not to be put to the test.

Then he withdrew from them, about a stone's throw away, and knelt down and prayed. 'Father,' he said, 'if you are willing, take this cup away from me. Nevertheless, let your will be done, not mine.' Then an angel appeared to him, coming from heaven to give him strength. In his anguish he prayed even more earnestly, and his sweat fell to the ground like great drops of blood.

When he rose from prayer he went to the disciples and found them sleeping for sheer grief. And he said to them, 'Why are you asleep? Get up and pray not to be put to the test.'

Reading from the Church's tradition

There is a state of resting in God, an absolute break from all intellectual activity, when one forms no plans, makes no decisions and for the first time really ceases to act, when one simply hands over the future to God's will and 'surrenders himself to fate'. I myself have experienced this state to some extent. It came in the wake of an experience which had overtaxed my strength, drained my spiritual resources and robbed me of the ability to act. Compared to that inertia arising from a lack of vital energy, 'resting in God' is something entirely new and distinct. One is a kind of 'stillness of death', whereas the other is marked by a sense of tremendous security.

Edith Stein, 'Psychic causality', p. 60

Concluding prayers

SATURDAY

Introductory prayer

Psalm 42, vv. 1–6

As a deer yearns
for running streams,
so I yearn
for you, my God.

I thirst for God,
the living God;
when shall I go to see
the face of God?

I have no food but tears
day and night,
as all day long I am taunted,
'Where is your God?'

This I remember
as I pour out my heart,
how I used to pass under the roof of the Most High
used to go to the house of God,
among cries of joy and praise,
the sound of the feast.

Why be so downcast,
why all these sighs?

Hope in God! I will praise him still,
my Saviour, my God.

When I am downcast
I think of you:
from the land of Jordan and Hermon,
I think of you, humble mountain.

Gospel reading: John 1.35-39

The next day as John stood there again with two of his disciples, Jesus went past, and John looked towards him and said, 'Look, there is the lamb of God.' And the two disciples heard what he said and followed Jesus. Jesus turned round, saw them following and said, 'What do you want?' They answered, 'Rabbi' – which means Teacher – 'where do you live?' He replied, 'Come and see'; so they went and saw where he lived, and stayed with him that day. It was about the tenth hour.

Reading from the Church's tradition

O great God of love, and Lord! How many riches do you place in the soul that neither loves nor is satisfied save in you alone, for you give yourself to it and become one with it through love. And consequently you give for its enjoyment and love what it most desires in you and what brings it most profit. But because it behoves us not to go without the cross, just as our Beloved did not go without it, even to the death of love, God ordains our sufferings that we may love what we most desire, make greater sacrifices, and be worth more. But everything is brief, for it lasts only until the knife is raised; and then Isaac remains alive with the promise of a multiplied offspring [Gn. 22:1-18].

John of the Cross, *The Letters*, letter 11, p. 745

Concluding prayers

SUNDAY

Introductory prayer

Psalm 49, vv. 1-2, 16-20
Hear this, all nations,
listen, all who dwell on earth,
people high and low,
rich and poor alike! . . .

Do not be overawed when someone gets rich,
and lives in ever greater splendour;
when he dies he will take nothing with him,
his wealth will not go down with him.

Though he pampered himself while he lived
– and people praise you for looking after yourself –
he will go to join the ranks of his ancestors,
who will never again see the light.

In prosperity people lose their good sense,
they become no better than dumb animals.

Gospel reading: Mark 6.45-52
And at once he made his disciples get into the boat and
go on ahead to the other side near Bethsaida, while he
himself sent the crowd away. After saying goodbye to
them he went off into the hills to pray. When evening
came, the boat was far out on the sea, and he was alone

on the land. He could see that they were hard pressed in their rowing, for the wind was against them; and about the fourth watch of the night he came towards them, walking on the sea. He was going to pass them by, but when they saw him walking on the sea they thought it was a ghost and cried out; for they had all seen him and were terrified. But at once he spoke to them and said, 'Courage! It's me! Don't be afraid.' Then he got into the boat with them and the wind dropped. They were utterly and completely dumbfounded, because they had not seen what the miracle of the loaves meant; their minds were closed.

Reading from the Church's tradition

As God brings the 'new man' to life in interior silence, that is to say, the new you, with the world view that Christ shares with you in deep silence, His view of things becomes more important to you than your own. Then He asks you to live that new life in the circumstances of everyday life, in your daily routine, contradicted by noise, opposition, and anxieties. These seem to persecute you because you want to be alone to relish that silence. But it is important to allow oneself to be confronted by daily life. The alternation between deep silence and action gradually brings the two together. You become fully integrated, a contemplative and yet fully capable of action at the same time. You are Mary and Martha at once.

Thomas Keating, *Open Mind, Open Heart*, p. 120

Concluding prayers

Week Three

MONDAY

Introductory prayer

Psalm 51, vv. 1–11

Have mercy on me, O God, in your faithful love,
in your great tenderness wipe away my offences;
wash me clean from my guilt,
purify me from my sin.

For I am well aware of my offences,
my sin is constantly in mind.
Against you, you alone, I have sinned,
I have done what you see to be wrong,

that you may show your saving justice when you pass
    sentence,
and your victory may appear when you give judgement,
remember, I was born guilty,
a sinner from the moment of conception.

But you delight in sincerity of heart,
and in secret you teach me wisdom.
Purify me with hyssop till I am clean,
wash me until I am whiter than snow.

Let me hear the sound of joy and gladness,
and the bones you have crushed will dance.
Turn away your face from my sins,
and wipe away all my guilt.

God, create in me a clean heart,
renew within me a resolute spirit,
do not thrust me away from your presence,
do not take away from me your spirit of holiness.

Gospel reading: Matthew 6.5–6

'And when you pray, do not imitate the hypocrites: they love to say their prayers standing up in the synagogues and at the street corners for people to see them. In truth I tell you, they have had their reward. But when you pray, *go to your private* room, shut yourself in, and so pray to your Father who is in that secret place, and your Father who sees all that is done in secret will reward you.'

Reading from the Church's tradition

Do not anticipate what will happen tomorrow. The same everlasting Father who cares for you today will take care of you tomorrow and every day. Either He will shield you from suffering or he will give you unfailing strength to bear it. Be at peace, then, and put aside all anxious thoughts and imaginations.

Francis de Sales, 'Do not look with fear', translator unknown

Concluding prayers

TUESDAY

Introductory prayer

Psalm 55, vv. 1-7, 22-23

God, hear my prayer,
do not hide away from my plea,
give me a hearing, answer me,
my troubles give me no peace.

I shudder at the enemy's shouts,
at the outcry of the wicked;
they heap up charges against me,
in their anger bring hostile accusations against me.

My heart writhes within me,
the terrors of death come upon me,
fear and trembling overwhelm me,
and shuddering grips me.

And I say,
'Who will give me wings like a dove,
to fly away and find rest?'
How far I would escape,
and make a nest in the desert! . . .

Unload your burden onto Yahweh
and he will sustain you;
never will he allow
the upright to stumble.

You, God, will thrust them down
to the abyss of destruction,
men bloodthirsty and deceptive,
before half their days are spent.

For my part, I put my trust in you.

Gospel reading: Luke 23.44–46

It was now about the sixth hour and the sun's light failed, so that darkness came over the whole land until the ninth hour. The veil of the Sanctuary was torn right down the middle. Jesus cried out in a loud voice saying, 'Father, *into your hands I commit my spirit.*' With these words he breathed his last.

Reading from the Church's tradition

Following Mary's example, the fundamental practice for healing the wounds of the false-self system is to fulfill the duties of our job in life. This includes helping people who are counting on us. If prayer gets in the way, there is some misunderstanding. Some devout persons think that if their activities at home or their job get in the way of praying, there is something wrong with their activities. On the contrary, there is something wrong with their prayer.

Thomas Keating, *The Mystery of Christ*, p. 24

Concluding prayers

WEDNESDAY

Introductory prayer

Psalm 57, vv. 1-7

Take pity on me, taken pity on me,
for in you I take refuge,
in the shadow of your wings I take refuge,
until the destruction is past.

I call to God the Most High,
to God who has done everything for me;
may he send from heaven and save me,
and check those who harry me;
may God send his faithful love and his constancy.

I lie surrounded by lions,
greedy for human prey,
their teeth are spears and arrows,
their tongue a sharp sword.

Be exalted above the heavens, God!
Your glory over all the earth!
They laid a snare in my path
– I was bowed with care –
they dug a pit ahead of me,
but fell in it themselves.

My heart is ready, God,
my heart is ready;
I will sing, and make music for you.

Gospel reading: Matthew 26.6-13

Jesus was at Bethany in the house of Simon, a man who had suffered from a virulent skin-disease, when a woman came to him with an alabaster jar of very expensive ointment, and poured it on his head as he was at table. When they saw this, the disciples said indignantly, 'Why this waste? This could have been sold for a high price and the money given to the poor.' But Jesus noticed this and said, 'Why are you upsetting the woman? What she has done for me is indeed a good work! You have the poor with you always, but you will not always have me. When she poured this ointment on my body, she did it to prepare me for burial. In truth I tell you, wherever in all the world this gospel is proclaimed, what she has done will be told as well, in remembrance of her.'

Reading from the Church's tradition

I was saying that the certainty of going away one day far from the sad and dark country had been given me from the day of my childhood. I did not believe this only because I heard it from persons much more knowledgeable than I, but I felt in the bottom of my heart real longings for this most beautiful country. Just as the genius of Christopher Columbus gave him a presentiment of a new world when nobody had even thought of such a thing; so also I felt that another land would one day serve me as a permanent dwelling place. Then suddenly the fog that surrounds me becomes more dense; it penetrates my soul and envelops it in such a way that it is impossible to discover within it the sweet image of my Fatherland; everything has disappeared! When I want to rest my heart fatigued by the darkness that surrounds it by the memory of the luminous country after which I aspire, my torment redoubles; it seems to me that the darkness, borrowing the voice of sinners, says mockingly to me: 'You are dreaming about the light, about a fatherland embalmed in the sweetest perfumes; you are dreaming about the *eternal* possession of the Creator of all these marvels; you believe that one day you will walk out of this fog that surrounds you! Advance, advance; rejoice in death which will give you not what you hope for but a night still more profound, the night of nothingness.'

Thérèse of Lisieux, *Story of a Soul*, p. 213

Concluding prayers

THURSDAY

Introductory prayer

Psalm 61
God, hear my cry,
listen to my prayer.
From the end of the earth I call to you
with fainting heart.
Lead me to the high rock that stands far
    out of my reach.

For you are my refuge,
a strong tower against the enemy.
Let me stay in your tent for ever,
taking refuge in the shelter of your wings!
For you, God, accept my vows,
you grant me the heritage of those who fear your name.

Let the king live on and on,
let his years continue age after age.
May his throne be always in God's presence,
your faithful love and constancy watch over him.
Then I shall always sing to your name,
day after day fulfilling my vows.

Gospel reading: Mark 6.7-13
Then he summoned the Twelve and began to send
them out in pairs, giving them authority over unclean

spirits. And he instructed them to take nothing for the journey except a staff – no bread, no haversack, no coppers for their purses. They were to wear sandals but, he added, 'Don't take a spare tunic.' And he said to them, 'If you enter a house anywhere, stay there until you leave the district. And if any place does not welcome you and people refuse to listen to you, as you walk away shake off the dust under your feet as evidence to them.' So they set off to proclaim repentance; and they cast out many devils, and anointed many sick people with oil and cured them.

Reading from the Church's tradition

One dark night,
fired with love's urgent longings
– ah, the sheer grace! –
I went out unseen,
my house being now all stilled.

In darkness, and secure,
by the secret ladder, disguised,
– ah, the sheer grace! –
in darkness and concealment,
my house being now all stilled.

On that glad night
in secret, for no one saw me,
nor did I look at anything
with no other light or guide

than the one that burned in my heart.

This guided me
more surely than the light of noon
to where he was awaiting me
– him I knew so well –
there in a place where no one appeared.

John of the Cross, 'The dark night',
stanzas 1–4, pp. 50–1

Concluding prayers

FRIDAY

Introductory prayer

Psalm 63

God, you are my God, I pine for you;
my heart thirsts for you,
my body longs for you,
as a land parched, dreary and waterless.
Thus I have gazed on you in the sanctuary,
seeing your power and your glory.

Better your faithful love than life itself;
my lips will praise you.
Thus I will bless you all my life,
in your name lift up my hands.
All my longings fulfilled as with fat and rich foods,
a song of joy on my lips and praise in my mouth.

On my bed when I think of you,
I muse on you in the watches of the night,
for you have always been my help;
in the shadow of your wings I rejoice;
my heart clings to you,
your right hand supports me.

May those who are hounding me to death
go down to the depths of the earth,
given over to the blade of the sword,

and left as food for jackals.
Then the king shall rejoice in God,
all who swear by him shall gain recognition,
for the mouths of liars shall be silenced.

Gospel reading: Luke 9.10-17

On their return the apostles gave him an account of all they had done. Then he took them with him and withdrew towards a town called Bethsaida where they could be by themselves. But the crowds got to know and they went after him. He made them welcome and talked to them about the kingdom of God; and he cured those who were in need of healing.

It was late afternoon when the Twelve came up to him and said, 'Send the people away, and they can go to the villages and farms round about to find lodging and food; for we are in a lonely place here.' He replied, 'Give them something to eat yourselves.' But they said, 'We have no more than five loaves and two fish, unless we are to go ourselves and buy food for all these people.' For there were about five thousand men. But he said to his disciples, 'Get them to sit down in parties of about fifty.' They did so and made them all sit down. Then he took the five loaves and the two fish, raised his eyes to heaven, and said the blessing over them; then he broke them and handed them to his disciples to distribute among the crowd. They all ate as much as they wanted, and when the scraps left over were collected they filled twelve baskets.

Reading from the Church's tradition

Now, then, the great good that it seems to me there will be in the kingdom of heaven, among many other blessings, is that one will no longer take any account of earthly things, but have a calmness and glory within, rejoice in the fact that all are rejoicing, experience perpetual peace and a wonderful inner satisfaction that comes from seeing that everyone hallows and praises the Lord and blesses His name and that no one offends Him. Everyone loves Him there, and the soul itself doesn't think about anything else than loving Him; nor can it cease loving Him, because it knows Him. And would that we could love Him in this way here below, even though we may not be able to do so with such perfection or stability. But if we knew him we would love in a way very different from that in which we do love Him.

Teresa of Avila, *The Way of Perfection*,
ch. 30, para. 5, p. 151

Concluding prayers

SATURDAY

Introductory prayer

Psalm 67
May God show kindness and bless us,
and make his face shine on us.
Then the earth will acknowledge your ways,
and all nations your power to save.

Let the nations praise you, God,
let all the nations praise you.

Let the nations rejoice and sing for joy,
for you judge the world with justice,
you judge the peoples with fairness,
you guide the nations on earth.

Let the nations praise you, God,
let all the nations praise you.

The earth has yielded its produce;
God, our God has blessed us.
May God continue to bless us,
and be revered by the whole wide world.

Gospel reading: John 10.14–18
'I am the good shepherd;
I know my own

and my own know me,
just as the Father knows me
and I know the Father;
and I lay down my life for my sheep.
And there are other sheep I have
that are not of this fold,
and I must lead these too.
They too will listen to my voice,
and there will be only one flock,
one shepherd.
The Father loves me,
because I lay down my life
in order to take it up again.
No one takes it from me;
I lay it down of my own free will,
and as I have power to lay it down,
so I have power to take it up again;
and this is the command
I have received from my Father.'

Reading from the Church's tradition

Suppose that through a practice like Centering Prayer, which prepares us for contemplation, the primary locus of the divine therapy, we take half an hour every day for solitude and silence, just to be with God and with ourselves (without knowing yet who that is). As a result of the deep rest and silence that come through such a practice, our emotional programs begin to be relativized. They were designed at a time when we didn't know the goodness and reassurance of God's presence. The presence of God is true security. There really isn't any other.

Thomas Keating, *The Human Condition*, pp. 31–2

Concluding prayers

SUNDAY

Introductory prayer

Psalm 72, vv. 1–8

God, endow the king with your own fair judgement,
the son of the king with your own saving justice,
that he may rule your people with justice,
and your poor with fair judgement.

Mountains and hills,
bring peace to the people!
With justice he will judge the poor of the people,
he will save the children of the needy
and crush their oppressors.

In the sight of the sun and the moon he will endure,
age after age.
He will come down like rain on mown grass,
like showers moistening the land.

In his days uprightness shall flourish,
and peace in plenty till the moon is no more.
His empire shall stretch from sea to sea,
from the river to the limits of the earth.

Gospel reading: Luke 10.38–42

In the course of their journey he came to a village, and
a woman named Martha welcomed him into her house.

She had a sister called Mary, who sat down at the Lord's feet and listened to him speaking. Now Martha, who was distracted with all the serving, came to him and said, 'Lord, do you not care that my sister is leaving me to do the serving all by myself? Please tell her to help me.' But the Lord answered, 'Martha, Martha,' he said, 'you worry and fret about so many things, and yet few are needed, indeed only one. It is Mary who has chosen the better part, and it is not to be taken from her.'

Reading from the Church's tradition

O guiding night!
O night more lovely than the dawn!
O night that has united
the Lover with his beloved,
transforming the beloved in her Lover.

Upon my flowering breast,
which I kept wholly for him alone,
there he lay sleeping,
and I caressing him
there in a breeze from the fanning cedars.

When the breeze blew from the turret,
as I parted his hair,
it wounded my neck
with its gentle hand,
suspending all my senses.

I abandoned and forgot myself,
laying my face on my Beloved;
all things ceased; I went out from myself,
leaving my cares
forgotten among the lilies.

> John of the Cross, 'The dark night',
> stanzas 5–8, pp. 51–2

Concluding prayers

Week Four

MONDAY

Introductory prayer

Psalm 76

God is acknowledged in Judah,
his name is great in Israel,
his tent is pitched in Salem,
his dwelling is in Zion;
there he has broken the lightning-flashes of the bow,
shield and sword and war.

Radiant you are, and renowned
for the mountains of booty taken from them.
Heroes are now sleeping their last sleep,
the warriors' arms have failed them;
at your reproof, God of Jacob,
chariot and horse stand stunned.

You, you alone, strike terror! Who can hold his ground
in your presence when your anger strikes?
From heaven your verdicts thunder,
the earth is silent with dread
when God takes his stand to give judgement,
to save all the humble of the earth.

Human anger serves only to praise you,
the survivors of your anger will huddle round you.
Make and fulfil your vows to Yahweh your God,
let those who surround him make offerings to the
      Awesome One.
He cuts short the breath of princes,
strikes terror in earthly kings.

Gospel reading: John 12.1-8

Six days before the Passover, Jesus went to Bethany,
were Lazarus was, whom he had raised from the dead.
They gave a dinner for him there; Martha waited on
them and Lazarus was among those at table. Mary
brought in a pound of very costly ointment, pure nard,
and with it anointed the feet of Jesus, wiping them with
her hair; the house was filled with the scent of the
ointment. Then Judas Iscariot – one of his disciples, the
man who was to betray him – said, 'Why was this
ointment not sold for three hundred denarii and the
money given to the poor?' He said this, not because he
cared about the poor, but because he was a thief; he
was in charge of the common fund and used to help
himself to the contents. So Jesus said, 'Leave her alone;
let her keep it for the day of my burial. You have the
poor with you always, you will not always have me.'

Reading from the Church's tradition

Lastly, look on the *great silence* of each evening with St
Benedict and the Fathers as a singular blessing. For

night is an immense mystery, bearer of the secret of
creation, incarnation, resurrection and the return that
will come at the dead of night. In this nocturnal silence,
watch and pray. God visits your heart in the night. Do
you, then, bless the Lord in the night. Desire him in the
night with your whole soul and let your spirit seek God
in silence, within. You sleep in peace, but your heart
keeps watch.

In the Heart of the City, In the Heart of God, pp. 30–1

Concluding prayers

TUESDAY

Introductory prayer

Psalm 77, vv. 1-9

I cry to God in distress,
I cry to God and he hears me.

In the day of my distress I sought the Lord;
all night I tirelessly stretched out my hands,
my heart refused to be consoled.
I sigh as I think of God,
my spirit faints away as I ponder on him.

You kept me from closing my eyes,
I was too distraught to speak;
I thought of former times,
years long past I recalled;
through the night I ponder in my heart,
as I reflect, my spirit asks this question:

Is the Lord's rejection final?
Will he never show favour again?
Is his faithful love gone for ever?
Has his Word come to an end for all time?
Does God forget to show mercy?
In anger does he shut off his tenderness?

Gospel reading: Matthew 14.15-21

When evening came, the disciples went to him and said, 'This is a lonely place, and time has slipped by; so send the people away, and they can go to the villages to buy themselves some food.' Jesus replied, 'There is no need for them to go: give them something to eat yourselves.' But they answered, 'All we have with us is five loaves and two fish.' So he said, 'Bring them here to me.' He gave orders that the people were to sit down on the grass; then he took the five loaves and the two fish, raised his eyes to heaven and said the blessing. And breaking the loaves he handed them to his disciples, who gave them to the crowds. They all ate as much as they wanted, and they collected the scraps left over, twelve baskets full. Now about five thousand men had eaten, to say nothing of women and children.

Reading from the Church's tradition

Prayer is looking up into the face of the Eternal. We can do this only when the spirit is awake in its innermost depths, freed from all earthly occupations and pleasures that numb it. Being awake in body does not guarantee this consciousness, nor does the rest required by nature interfere.

Edith Stein, *The Hidden Life*, pp. 3–4

Concluding prayers

WEDNESDAY

Introductory prayer

Psalm 80, vv. 1–7
Shepherd of Israel, listen,
you who lead Joseph like a flock,
enthroned on the winged creatures, shine forth
over Ephraim, Benjamin and Manasseh;
rouse your valour
and come to our help.

God, bring us back,
let your face shine on us and we shall be safe.

Yahweh, God Sabaoth, how long
will you flare up at your people's prayer?
You have made tears their food,
redoubled tears their drink.
You let our neighbours quarrel over us,
our enemies mock us.

God Sabaoth, bring us back,
let your face shine on us and we shall be safe.

Gospel reading: Mark 14.22–25
And as they were eating he took bread, and when he
had said the blessing he broke it and gave it to them.
'Take it,' he said, 'this is my body.' Then he took a cup,

and when he had given thanks he handed it to them, and all drank from it, and he said to them, 'This is my blood, the blood of the covenant, poured out for many. In truth I tell you, I shall never drink wine any more until the day I drink the new wine in the kingdom of God.'

Reading from the Church's tradition

We are living now in an age of inventions, and we no longer have to take the trouble of climbing stairs, for, in the homes of the rich, an elevator has replaced these very successfully. I wanted to find an elevator which would raise me to Jesus, for I am too small to climb the rough stairway of perfection. I searched, then, in the Scriptures for some sign of this elevator, the object of my desires, and I read these words coming from the mouth of Eternal Wisdom: "*Whoever is a LITTLE ONE, let him come to me.*" And so I succeeded. I felt I had found what I was looking for. But wanting to know, O my God, what you would do to *the very little one* who answered Your call, I continued my search and this is what I discovered: "*As one whom a mother caresses, so will I comfort you; you shall be carried at the breasts, and upon the knees they shall caress you.*" Ah! never did words more tender and more melodious come to give joy to my soul. The elevator which must raise me to heaven is Your arms, O Jesus! And for this I had no need to grow up, but

rather I had to remain *little* and become this more
and more.

Thérèse of Lisieux, *Story of a Soul*, pp. 207–8

Concluding prayers

THURSDAY

Introductory prayer

Psalm 84, vv. 1-5
How lovely are your dwelling-places,
Yahweh Sabaoth.
My whole being yearns and pines
for Yahweh's courts,
My heart and my body cry out for joy
to the living God.

Even the sparrow has found a home,
the swallow a nest to place its young:
your altars, Yahweh Sabaoth,
my King and my God.

How blessed are those who live in your house;
they shall praise you continually.
Blessed those who find their strength in you,
whose hearts are set on pilgrimage.

Gospel reading: John 12.35-36
Jesus then said:
The light will be with you
only a little longer now.
Go on your way while you have the light,
or darkness will overtake you,
and nobody who walks in the dark

knows where he is going.
While you still have the light,
believe in the light
so that you may become children of light.

Reading from the Church's tradition

This way of life contains very little business and bustling, and demands mortification of the will more than knowledge. The less one takes of things and pleasures the farther one advances along this way.

Think not that pleasing God lies so much in doing a great deal as in doing it with good will, without possessiveness and human respect.

When evening comes, you will be examined in love. Learn to love as God desires to be loved and abandon your own ways of acting.

John of the Cross, *The Sayings of Light and Love*,
nos 58–60, p. 90

Concluding prayers

FRIDAY

Introductory prayer

Psalm 86, vv. 1-8

Listen to me, Yahweh, answer me,
for I am poor and needy.
Guard me, for I am faithful,
save your servant who relies on you.

You are my God, take pity on me, Lord,
for to you I cry all the day.
Fill your servant's heart with joy, Lord,
for to you I raise up my heart.

Lord, you are kind and forgiving,
rich in faithful love for all who call upon you.
Yahweh, hear my prayer,
listen to the sound of my pleading.

In my day of distress I call upon you,
because you answer me, Lord;
among the gods there is none to compare with you,
no great deeds to compare with yours.

Gospel reading: Mark 8.34-38

He called the people and his disciples to him and said,
'If anyone wants to be a follower of mine, let him
renounce himself and take up his cross and follow me.

Anyone who wants to save his life will lose it; but anyone who loses his life for my sake, and for the sake of the gospel, will save it. What gain, then, is it for anyone to win the whole world and forfeit his life? And indeed, what can anyone offer in exchange for his life? For if anyone in this sinful and adulterous generation is ashamed of me and my words, the Son of man will also be ashamed of him when he comes in the glory of his Father with the holy angels.'

Reading from the Church's tradition

Contemplative prayer enables us to see the treasures of sanctification and the opportunities for spiritual growth that are present day by day in ordinary life. If one is transformed, one can walk down the street, drink a cup of tea or shake hands with somebody and be pouring divine life into the world. In Christianity motivation is everything. When the love of Christ is the principal motivation, ordinary actions transmit divine love. This is the fundamental Christian witness; this is evangelization in its primary form.

Thomas Keating, *The Mystery of Christ*, pp. 24–5

Concluding prayers

SATURDAY

Introductory prayer

Psalm 88, vv. 1−9

Yahweh, God of my salvation,
when I cry out to you in the night,
may my prayer reach your presence,
hear my cry for help.

For I am filled with misery,
my life is on the brink of Sheol;
already numbered among those who sink into
    oblivion,
I am as one bereft of strength,
left alone among the dead,
like the slaughtered lying in the grave,
whom you remember no more,
cut off as they are from your protection.

You have plunged me to the bottom of the grave,
in the darkness, in the depths;
weighted down by your anger,
kept low by your waves.

You have deprived me of my friends,
made me repulsive to them,
imprisoned, with no escape;
my eyes are worn out with suffering.

I call to you, Yahweh, all day,
I stretch out my hands to you.

Gospel reading: Matthew 20.1–16

'Now the kingdom of Heaven is like a landowner going out at daybreak to hire workers for his vineyard. He made an agreement with the workers for one denarius a day and sent them to his vineyard. Going out at about the third hour he saw others standing idle in the market place and said to them, "You go to my vineyard too and I will give you a fair wage." So they went. At about the sixth hour and again at about the ninth hour, he went out and did the same. Then at about the eleventh hour he went out and found more men standing around, and he said to them, "Why have you been standing here idle all day?" "Because no one has hired us," they answered. He said to them, "You go into my vineyard too." In the evening, the owner of the vineyard said to his bailiff, "Call the workers and pay them their wages, starting with the last arrivals and ending with the first." So those who were hired at about the eleventh hour came forward and received one denarius each. When the first came, they expected to get more, but they too received one denarius each. They took it, but grumbled at the landowner saying, "The men who came last have done only one hour, and you have treated them the same as us, though we have done a heavy day's work in all the heat." He answered one of them and said, "My friend, I am not being unjust to you; did we not agree on one denarius? Take your earnings and go. I choose to pay the lastcomer as much as I pay you. Have I no right to do what I like with my own? Why should you be envious because I am generous?" Thus the last will be first, and the first, last.'

Reading from the Church's tradition
One day while I was anxiously desiring to help the order, the Lord told me: "Do what lies in your power; surrender yourself to me; and do not be disturbed about anything; rejoice in the good that has been given you, for it is very great; my Father takes His delight in you, and the Holy Spirit loves you."

Teresa of Avila, *Spiritual Testimonies*, no. 10, p. 388

Concluding prayers

SUNDAY

Introductory prayer

Psalm 90, vv. 1-8

Lord, you have been our refuge
from age to age.

Before the mountains were born,
before the earth and the world came to birth,
from eternity to eternity you are God.

You bring human beings to the dust,
by saying, 'Return, children of Adam,'
A thousand years are to you
like a yesterday which has passed,
like a watch of the night.

You flood them with sleep
– in the morning they will be like growing grass:
in the morning it is blossoming and growing,
by evening it is withered and dry.

For we have been destroyed by your wrath,
dismayed by your anger.
You have taken note of our guilty deeds,
our secrets in the full light of your presence.

Gospel reading: Luke 7.36-50

One of the Pharisees invited him to a meal. When he arrived at the Pharisee's house and took his place at table, suddenly a woman came in, who had a bad name in the town. She had heard he was dining with the Pharisee and had brought with her an alabaster jar of ointment. She waited behind him at his feet, weeping, and her tears fell on his feet, and she wiped them away with her hair; then she covered his feet with kisses and anointed them with the ointment.

When the Pharisee who had invited him saw this, he said to himself, 'If this man were a prophet, he would know who this woman is and what sort of person it is who is touching him and what a bad name she has.' Then Jesus took him up and said, 'Simon, I have something to say to you.' He replied, 'Say on, Master.' 'There was once a creditor who had two men in his debt; one owed him five hundred denarii, the other fifty. They were unable to pay, so he let them both off. Which of them will love him more?' Simon answered, 'The one who was let off more, I suppose.' Jesus said, 'You are right.'

Then he turned to the woman and said to Simon, 'You see this woman? I came into your house, and you poured no water over my feet, but she has poured out her tears over my feet and wiped them away with her hair. You gave me no kiss, but she has been covering my feet with kisses ever since I came in. You did not anoint my head with oil, but she has anointed my feet with ointment. For this reason I tell you that her sins, many as they are, have been forgiven her, because she has shown such great love. It is someone who is forgiven little who shows little love.' Then he said to her, 'Your sins are forgiven.' Those who were with him at table began to say to themselves, 'Who is this man, that even forgives sins?' But he said to the woman, 'Your faith has saved you; go in peace.'

Reading from the Church's tradition

We can offer three reasons for calling the journey toward union with God a night.

The first has to do with the point of departure, because individuals must deprive themselves of their appetites for worldly possessions. This denial and privation is like a night for all one's senses.

The second reason refers to the means or the road along which a person travels to this union. Now this road is faith, and for the intellect faith is also like a dark night.

The third reason pertains to the point of arrival, namely God. And God is also a dark night to the soul in this life. These three nights pass through a soul, or better, the soul passes through them in order to reach union with God.

John of the Cross, *The Ascent of Mount Carmel*,
bk 1, ch. 2, para. 1, p. 120

Concluding prayers

Week 5

MONDAY

Introductory prayer

Psalm 91, vv. 1-9

You who live in the secret places of Elyon,
spend your nights in the shelter of Shaddai,
saying to Yahweh, 'My refuge, my fortress,
my God in whom I trust!'

He rescues you from the snare
of the fowler set on destruction;
he covers you with his pinions,
you find shelter under his wings.
His constancy is shield and protection.

You need not fear the terrors of night,
the arrow that flies in the daytime,
the plague that stalks in the darkness,
the scourge that wreaks havoc at high noon.

Though a thousand fall at your side,
ten thousand at your right hand,
you yourself will remain unscathed.
You have only to keep your eyes open

to see how the wicked are repaid,
you who say, 'Yahweh my refuge!'
and make Elyon your fortress.

Gospel reading: Matthew 26.20–25

When evening came he was at table with the Twelve.
And while they were eating he said, 'In truth I tell you,
one of you is about to betray me.' They were greatly
distressed and started asking him in turn, 'Not me,
Lord, surely?' He answered, 'Someone who has dipped
his hand into the dish with me will betray me. The Son
of man is going to his fate, as the scriptures say he will,
but alas for that man by whom the Son of man is
betrayed! Better for that man if he had never been
born!' Judas, who was to betray him, asked in his turn,
'Not me, Rabbi, surely?' Jesus answered, 'It is you who
say it.'

Reading from the Church's tradition

After earth's Exile, I hope to go and enjoy you in the
Fatherland, but I do not want to lay up merits for
heaven. I want to work for Your *Love alone* with the one
purpose of pleasing You, consoling your Sacred Heart,
and saving souls who will love You eternally.

In the evening of this life, I shall appear before You
with empty hands, for I do not ask You, Lord, to count
my works. All our justice is stained in Your eyes. I wish,
then, to be clothed in Your own *Justice* and to receive
from Your *Love* the eternal possession of *Yourself*. I

want no other *Throne*, no other *Crown* but *You*, my *Beloved*!

Time is nothing in Your eyes, and a single day is like a thousand years. You can, then, in one instant prepare me to appear before You.

Thérèse of Lisieux, 'Act of oblation to Merciful Love', pp. 254–5

Concluding prayers

TUESDAY

Introductory prayer

Psalm 92, vv. 1-8
It is good to give thanks to Yahweh,
to make music for your name, Most High,
to proclaim your faithful love at daybreak,
and your constancy all through the night,
on the lyre, the ten-stringed lyre,
to the murmur of the harp.

You have brought me joy, Yahweh, by your deeds,
at the work of your hands I cry out,
'How great are your works, Yahweh,
immensely deep your thoughts!'
Stupid people cannot realize this,
fools do not grasp it.

The wicked may sprout like weeds,
and every evil-doer flourish,
but only to be eternally destroyed;
whereas you are supreme for ever, Yahweh.

Gospel reading: Mark 2.15-17
When Jesus was at dinner in his house, a number of tax
collectors and sinners were also sitting at table with
Jesus and his disciples; for there were many of them
among his followers. When the scribes of the Pharisee

party saw him eating with sinners and tax collectors, they said to his disciples, 'Why does he eat with tax collectors and sinners?' When Jesus heard this he said to them, 'It is not the healthy who need the doctor, but the sick. I came to call not the upright, but sinners.'

Reading from the Church's tradition

Once a regular practice of Centering Prayer has been established, we move normally in each period of prayer toward a place of rest where our faculties are relatively calm and quiet. Thoughts are coming downstream, but as we learn to disregard them, we begin to enjoy a sense of the divine presence. Beyond our thinking and emotional experience is the deeper reality of the spiritual level of our being. It is another way of knowing reality that is unlike ordinary psychological awareness. As a result, not only is the mind quiet and at rest from the ordinary concerns of daily life, but the body also begins to rest, a rest that is deeper than sleep.

Thomas Keating, *The Human Condition*, pp. 33–4

Concluding prayers

WEDNESDAY

Introductory prayer

Psalm 104, vv. 1–4, 19–23
Bless Yahweh, my soul,
Yahweh, my God, how great you are!
Clothed in majesty and splendour,
wearing the light as a robe!

You stretch our the heavens like a tent,
build your palace on the waters above,
making the clouds your chariot,
gliding on the wings of the wind,
appointing the winds your messengers,
flames of fire your servants. . . .

He made the moon to mark the seasons,
the sun knows when to set.
You bring on darkness, and night falls,
when all the forest beasts roam around;
young lions roar for their prey,
asking God for their food.

Gospel reading: Luke 21.37–38
All day long he would be in the Temple teaching, but
would spend the night in the open on the hill called the
Mount of Olives. And from early morning the people
thronged to him in the Temple to listen to him.

Reading from the Church's tradition

I don't mean that these appeals and calls are like the ones I shall speak of later on. But they come through words spoken by other good people, or through sermons, or through what is read in good books, or through the many things that are heard and by which God calls, or through illnesses and trials, or also through a truth that he teaches during the brief moments we spend in prayer; however lukewarm these moments may be, God esteems them highly. And you, Sisters, don't underestimate this first favour, nor should you become disconsolate if you don't respond at once to the Lord. His Majesty knows well how to wait many days and years, especially when He sees perseverance and good desires. This perseverance is most necessary here. One always gains much through perseverance.

Teresa of Avila, *The Interior Castle*, pt 2, ch. 1, p. 298

Concluding prayers

THURSDAY

Introductory prayer

Psalm 107, vv. 1-5, 10-14
Alleluia!

Give thanks to Yahweh for he is good,
his faithful love lasts for ever.

So let them say whom Yahweh redeemed,
whom he redeemed from the power of their enemies,
bringing them back from foreign lands,
from east and west, north and south.

They were wandering in the desert, in the wastelands,
could find no way to an inhabited city;
they were hungry and thirsty,
their life was ebbing away. . . .

Sojourners in gloom and shadow dark as death,
fettered in misery and chains,
for defying the orders of Yahweh,
for scorning the plan of the Most High –
he subdued their spirit by hard labour;
if they fell there was no one to help.

They cried out to Yahweh in their distress,
he rescued them from their plight,

he brought them out from gloom and shadow
   dark as death,
and shattered their chains.

Gospel reading: John 1.1-5

In the beginning was the Word:
the Word was with God
and the Word was God.
He was with God in the beginning.
Through him all things came into being,
not one thing came into being
except through him.
What has come into being in him was life,
life that was the light of men;
and light shines in darkness,
and darkness could not overpower it.

Reading from the Church's tradition

The habit of referring everything to God and of flying
to him for refuge, together with the experience of being
delivered, has brought us a profound stability of soul.
It is the Sabbath rest, of which Sunday is the symbol,
and of which heaven is the perfect fulfilment. . . . The
fullness of love brings the maximum of rest at the same
time that it makes possible the maximum of action.
Mary, the mother of Jesus, is the exemplar of this
grace. That is why, on the feast of the Assumption in
the Cistercian liturgy, the gospel of Mary and Martha
is read. As the perfect contemplative, she unites in

herself the capacity to work for God and to rest in God, which belongs to those who have passed through the crisis of faith and of love, and who have entered interiorly into the Sabbath of the Lord.

Thomas Keating, *Crisis of Faith, Crisis of Love*, p. 94

Concluding prayers

FRIDAY

Introductory prayer

Psalm 112
Alleluia!

How blessed is anyone who fears Yahweh,
who delights in his commandments!
His descendants shall be powerful on earth,
the race of the honest shall receive blessings:

Riches and wealth for his family;
his uprightness stands firm for ever.
For the honest he shines as a lamp in the dark,
generous, tender-hearted, and upright.

All goes well for one who lends generously,
who is honest in all his dealing;
for all time to come he will not stumble,
for all time to come the upright will be
     remembered.

Bad news holds no fears for him,
firm is his heart, trusting in Yahweh.
His heart held steady, he has no fears,
till he can gloat over his enemies.

To the needy he gives without stint,
his uprightness stands firm for ever;
his reputation is founded on strength.

The wicked are vexed at the sight,
they grind their teeth and waste away.
The desires of the wicked will be frustrated.

Gospel reading: Luke 9.57-62

As they travelled along they met a man on the road who
said to him, 'I will follow you wherever you go.' Jesus
answered, 'Foxes have holes and the birds of the air
have nests, but the Son of man has nowhere to lay his
head.'

Another to whom he said, 'Follow me,' replied,
'Let me go and bury my father first.' But he
answered, 'Leave the dead to bury their dead; your
duty is to go and spread the news of the kingdom of
God.'

Another said, 'I will follow you, sir, but first let me
go and say good-bye to my people at home.' Jesus
said to him, 'Once the hand is laid on the plough, no
one who looks back is fit for the kingdom of God.'

Reading from the Church's tradition

the tranquil night
In this spiritual sleep in the bosom of the Beloved, the
soul possesses and relishes all the tranquility, rest, and
quietude of the peaceful night; and she receives in God,

together with this peace, a fathomless and obscure divine knowledge. As a result she says that her Beloved is a tranquil night to her.

John of the Cross, *The Spiritual Canticle*, commentary on stanzas 14 and 15, para. 22, p. 534

Concluding prayers

SATURDAY

Introductory prayer

Psalm 119, vv. 55-64

All night, Yahweh, I hold your name in mind
I keep your Law.
This is what it means to me,
observing your precepts.

My task, I have said, Yahweh,
is to keep your word.
Wholeheartedly I entreat your favour
true to your promise, take pity on me!
I have reflected on my ways,
and I turn my steps to your instructions.
I hurry without delay
to keep your commandments.
Though caught in the snares of the wicked,
I do not forget your Law.
At midnight I rise to praise you
for your upright judgements.
I am a friend to all who fear you
and keep your precepts.
Your faithful love fills the earth,
Yahweh, teach me your judgements.

Gospel reading: Matthew 10.26–33

'So do not be afraid of them. Everything now covered up will be uncovered, and everything now hidden will be made clear. What I say to you in the dark, tell in the daylight; what you hear in whispers, proclaim from the housetops.

'Do not be afraid of those who kill the body but cannot kill the soul; fear him rather who can destroy both body and soul in hell. Can you not buy two sparrows for a penny? And yet not one falls to the ground without your Father knowing. Why, every hair on your head has been counted. So there is no need to be afraid; you are worth more than many sparrows.

'So if anyone declares himself for me in the presence of human beings, I will declare myself for him in the presence of my Father in heaven. But the one who disowns me in the presence of human beings, I will disown in the presence of my Father in heaven.

Reading from the Church's tradition

It is no hardship for me to introduce this book by Pierre-Marie Delfieux. . . .

Delfieux chose the city and went to Paris, where he pitched his tent. But his heart was in the desert.

I chose the desert sands, but my heart was in the city.

With Pierre-Marie's project in mind, I wrote the book *The Desert in the City*, explaining what a fine thing founding the Monastic Communities of Jerusalem would be.

The root was the same, and we were consciously united in the same cause.

Every evening at the hour of incense, I found myself, in spirit, saying Vespers with him in Paris, while he, in spirit, joined me 'in silent prayer and adoration' at Our Lady of the Dunes in Beni Abbes.

'Foreword' by Carlo Carretto, in *In the Heart of the City, In the Heart of God*, pp. vii–viii

Concluding prayers

SUNDAY

Introductory prayer

Psalm 121

I lift up my eyes to the mountains;
where is my help to come from?
My help comes from Yahweh
who made heaven and earth.

May he save your foot from stumbling;
may he, your guardian, not fall asleep!
You see – he neither sleeps nor slumbers,
the guardian of Israel.

Yahweh is your guardian, your shade,
Yahweh, at your right hand.
By day the sun will not strike you,
nor the moon by night.

Yahweh guards you from all harm
Yahweh guards your life,
Yahweh guards your comings and goings,
henceforth and for ever.

Gospel reading: John 19.25–27

Near the cross of Jesus stood his mother and his
mother's sister, Mary the wife of Clopas, and Mary of
Magdala. Seeing his mother and the disciple whom he

loved standing near her, Jesus said to his mother, 'Woman, this is your son.' Then to the disciple he said, 'This is your mother.' And from that hour the disciple took her into his home.

Reading from the Church's tradition

Mary entered the house of Elizabeth and said hello. The Presence that she carried within her was transmitted to Elizabeth by the sound of her voice. In response, the baby in Elizabeth's womb leapt for joy; he was sanctified by Mary's simple greeting. God's greatest works take place without our doing anything spectacular. They are almost side-effects of doing the ordinary things we are supposed to be doing. If you are transformed, everybody in your life will be changed too. There is a sense in which we create the world in which we live. If you are pouring out love everywhere you go, that love will start coming back; it cannot be otherwise. The more you give, the more you will receive.

Thomas Keating, *The Mystery of Christ*, p. 24

Concluding prayers

Week Six

MONDAY

Introductory prayer

Psalm 127
If Yahweh does not build a house
in vain do its builders toil.
If Yahweh does not guard a city
in vain does its guard keep watch.

In vain you get up earlier,
and put off going to bed,
sweating to make a living,
since it is he who provides for his beloved as they sleep.

Sons are a birthright from Yahweh,
children are a reward from him.
Like arrows in a warrior's hand
are the sons you father when young.

How blessed is the man
who has filled his quiver with them;
in dispute with his enemies at the city gate
he will not be worsted.

Gospel reading: Mark 15.42–47

It was now evening, and since it was Preparation Day – that is, the day before the Sabbath – there came Joseph of Arimathaea, a prominent member of the Council, who himself lived in the hope of seeing the kingdom of God, and he boldly went to Pilate and asked for the body of Jesus. Pilate, astonished that he should have died so soon, summoned the centurion and enquired if he had been dead for some time. Having been assured of this by the centurion, he granted the corpse to Joseph who bought a shroud, took Jesus down from the cross, wrapped him in the shroud and laid him in a tomb which had been hewn out of the rock. He then rolled a stone against the entrance to the tomb. Mary of Magdala and Mary the mother of Joset took note of where he was laid.

Reading from the Church's tradition

Now, then, the great good that it seems to me there will be in the kingdom of heaven, among many other blessings, is that one will no longer take any account of earthly things, but have a calmness and glory within, rejoice in the fact that all are rejoicing, experience perpetual peace and a wonderful inner satisfaction that comes from seeing that everyone hallows and praises the Lord and blesses His name and that no one offends Him. Everyone loves Him there, and the soul itself doesn't think about anything else than loving Him; nor can it cease loving Him, because it knows Him.

> Teresa of Avila, *The Way of Perfection*,
> ch. 30, para. 5, p. 151

Concluding prayers

TUESDAY

Introductory prayer

Psalm 131
Yahweh, my heart is not haughty,
I do not set my sights too high.
I have taken no part in great affairs,
in wonders beyond my scope.
No, I hold myself in quiet and silence,
like a little child in its mother's arms,
like a little child, so I keep myself.
Let Israel hope in Yahweh
henceforth and for ever.

Gospel reading: John 4.7-14
When a Samaritan woman came to draw water, Jesus
said to her, 'Give me something to drink.' His disciples
had gone into the town to buy food. The Samaritan
woman said to him, 'You are a Jew. How is it that you
ask me, a Samaritan, for something to drink?' – Jews,
of course, do not associate with Samaritans. Jesus
replied to her:

If you only knew what God is offering
and who it is that is saying to you,
'Give me something to drink,'
you would have been the one to ask,
and he would have given you living water.

'You have no bucket, sir,' she answered, and the well is deep: how do you get this living water? Are you a greater man than our father Jacob, who gave us this well and drank from it himself with his sons and his cattle?' Jesus replied:

Whoever drinks this water
will be thirsty again;
but no one who drinks the water that I shall give
will ever be thirsty again:
the water that I shall give
will become a spring of water within, welling up for
eternal life.

Reading from the Church's tradition

O Jesus, Your *little bird* is happy to be *weak and little*. What would become of it if it were big? Never would it have the boldness to appear in Your presence, *to fall asleep* in front of You. Yes, this is still one of the weaknesses of the little bird: when it wants to fix its gaze upon the Divine Sun, and when the clouds prevent it from seeing a single ray of that Sun, in spite of itself, its little eyes close, its little head is hidden beneath its wing, and the poor little thing falls asleep, believing all the time that it is fixing its gaze upon its Dear Star. When it awakens, it doesn't feel desolate; its little heart is at peace and it begins once again its work of *love*. It calls upon the angels and saints who rise like eagles before the consuming Fire, and since this is the object of the little bird's desire the eagles take pity on it, protecting and defending it, and putting to flight at the same time the vultures who want to devour it. These vultures are the demons whom the little bird doesn't fear, for it is not destined to be their *prey* but the prey of the *Eagle* whom it contemplates in the center of the Sun of Love.

Thérèse of Lisieux, *Story of a Soul*, p. 199

Concluding prayers

WEDNESDAY

Introductory prayer

Psalm 136, vv. 1-9
Alleluia!

Give thanks to Yahweh for he is good,
for his faithful love endures for ever.
Give thanks to the God of gods,
for his faithful love endures for ever.
Give thanks to the Lord of lords,
for his faithful love endures for ever.

He alone works wonders,
for his faithful love endures for ever.
In wisdom he made the heavens,
for his faithful love endures for ever.
He set the earth firm on the waters,
for his faithful love endures for ever.

He made the great lights,
for his faithful love endures for ever.
The sun to rule the day,
for his faithful love endures for ever.
Moon and stars to rule the night,
for his faithful love endures for ever.

Gospel reading: Mark 10.28-31

Peter took this up. 'Look,' he said to him [Jesus], 'we have left everything and followed you.' Jesus said, 'In truth I tell you, there is no one who has left house, brothers, sisters, mother, father, children or land for my sake and for the sake of the gospel who will not receive a hundred times as much, houses, brothers, sisters, mothers, children and land – and persecutions too – now in this present time and, in the world to come, eternal life. Many who are first will be last, and the last, first.'

Reading from the Church's tradition

silent music,

In that nocturnal tranquility and silence and in knowledge of the divine light the soul becomes aware of Wisdom's wonderful harmony and sequence in the variety of her creatures and works. Each of them is endowed with a certain likeness of God and in its own way gives voice to what God is in it. So creatures will be for the soul a harmonious symphony of sublime music surpassing all concerts and melodies of the world. She calls this music 'silent' because it is tranquil and quiet knowledge, without the sound of voices. And thus there is in it the sweetness of music and the quietude of silence. Accordingly, she says that her Beloved is silent music because in him she knows and enjoys this symphony of spiritual music. Not only is he silent music, but he is also

Sounding solitude.

> John of the Cross, *The Spiritual Canticle*,
> commentary on stanzas 14 and 15,
> para. 25, pp. 535–6

Concluding prayers

THURSDAY

Introductory prayer

Psalm 139, vv. 1-6, 9-12

Yahweh, you examine me and know me,
you know when I sit, when I rise,
you understand my thoughts from afar.
You watch when I walk or lie down,
you know every detail of my conduct.

A word is not yet on my tongue
before you, Yahweh, know all about it.
You fence me in, behind and in front,
you have laid your hand upon me.
Such amazing knowledge is beyond me,
a height to which I cannot attain. . . .

If I speed away on the wings of the dawn,
if I dwell beyond the ocean,
even there your hand will be guiding me,
your right hand holding me fast.

I will say, 'Let the darkness cover me,
and the night wrap itself around me,'
even darkness to you is not dark,
and night is as clear as the day.

Gospel reading: Matthew 8.16-17

That evening they brought him many who were possessed by devils. He drove out the spirits with a command and cured all who were sick. This was to fulfil what was spoken by the prophet Isaiah:

He himself bore our sicknesses away
and carried our diseases.

Reading from the Church's tradition

The first stage of your Passover of poverty is the *humble acceptance of your wealth.*

No matter what you do or say, you are rich in your faith, hope, love of the community, your culture, health, freedom and even in knowing why you thirst for poverty. Do not let this make you feel either ashamed or vain; God has no favorites. Do not feel guilty about it, but never forget it.

In return continually thank God and, since you have nothing that you have not received, let poverty lead you to offer a ceaseless sacrifice of praise. Live humbly, for you may not glory in what comes from God alone and not from you. Nor can you foresee to what hiddenness and deprivation God may want to lead you tomorrow, in the steps of the One who was brought to nothing for our sake. Be ready, then, and thankful, and you will have taken the first step into the mystery of poverty.

In the Heart of the City, In the Heart of God, p. 66

Concluding prayers

FRIDAY

Introductory prayer

Psalm 141
Yahweh, I am calling, hurry to me,
listen to my voice when I call to you.
May my prayer be like incense in your presence,
my uplifted hands like the evening sacrifice.

Yahweh, mount a guard over my mouth,
a guard at the door of my lips.
Check any impulse to speak evil,
to share the foul deeds of evil-doers.

I shall not sample their delights!
May the upright correct me with a friend's rebuke;
but the wicked shall never anoint my head with oil,
for that would make me party to their crimes.

They are delivered into the power of the rock,
    their judge,
those who took pleasure in hearing me say,
'Like a shattered millstone on the ground
our bones are scattered at the mouth of Sheol.'

To you, Yahweh, I turn my eyes,
in you I take refuge, do not leave me
    unprotected.

Save me from the traps that are set for me,
the snares of evil-doers.

Let the wicked fall each into his own net,
while I pass on my way.

Gospel reading: Luke 2.1−12

Now it happened that at this time Caesar Augustus
issued a decree that a census should be made of the
whole inhabited world. This census – the first – took
place while Quirinius was governor of Syria, and
everyone went to be registered, each to his own town.
So Joseph set out from the town of Nazareth in Galilee
for Judaea, to David's town called Bethlehem, since
he was of David's House and line, in order to be
registered together with Mary, his betrothed, who
was with child. Now it happened that, while they were
there, the time came for her to have her child, and she
gave birth to a son, her first-born. She wrapped him
in swaddling clothes and laid him in a manger because
there was no room for them in the living-space. In the
countryside close by there were shepherds out in the
fields keeping guard over their sheep during the
watches of the night. An angel of the Lord stood over
them and the glory of the Lord shone round them.
They were terrified, but the angel said, 'Do not be
afraid. Look, I bring you news of great joy, a joy to be
shared by the whole people. Today in the town of
David a Saviour has been born to you; he is Christ the

Lord. And here is a sign for you: you will find a baby wrapped in swaddling clothes and lying in a manger.'

Reading from the Church's tradition

A great aid to going against your will is to bear in mind continually how all is vanity and how quickly everything comes to an end. This helps to remove our attachment to trivia and center it on what will never end. Even though this practice seems to be a weak means, it will strengthen the soul greatly, and the soul will be most careful in very little things. When we begin to be attached to something, we should strive to turn our thoughts from it and bring them back to God – and His Majesty helps. He has done us a great favor because in this house most of the work of detachment has been done – although this turning and being against ourselves is a difficult thing because we live very close together and love ourselves greatly.

Teresa of Avila, *The Way of Perfection*,
ch. 10, para. 2, p. 76

Concluding prayers

SATURDAY

Introductory prayer

Psalm 146

Alleluia!
Praise Yahweh, my soul!
I will praise Yahweh all my life,
I will make music to my God as long as I live.

Do not put your trust in princes,
in any child of Adam, who has no power to save.
When his spirit goes forth he returns to the earth,
on that very day all his plans come to nothing.

How blessed is he who has Jacob's God to help him,
his hope is in Yahweh his God,
who made heaven and earth,
the sea and all that is in them.

He keeps faith for ever,
gives justice to the oppressed,
gives food to the hungry;
Yahweh sets prisoners free.

Yahweh gives sight to the blind,
lifts up those who are bowed down.
Yahweh protects the stranger,
he sustains the orphan and the widow.

Yahweh loves the upright,
but he frustrates the wicked.
Yahweh reigns for ever,
your God, Zion, from age to age.

Gospel reading: Mark 9.33-37

They came to Capernaum, and when he got into the
house he asked them, 'What were you arguing about
on the road? They said nothing, because on the road
they had been arguing which of them was the greatest.
So he sat down, called the Twelve to him and said, 'If
anyone wants to be first, he must make himself last of
all and servant of all.' He then took a little child whom
he set among them and embraced, and he said to them,
'Anyone who welcomes a little child such as this in my
name, welcomes me; and anyone who welcomes me,
welcomes not me but the one who sent me.'

Reading from the Church's tradition

Don't think this union is some kind of dreamy state like
the one I mentioned before. I say "dreamy state"
because it only seems that the soul is asleep; for neither
does it really think it is asleep nor does it feel awake.
There is no need here to use any technique to suspend
the mind since all the faculties are asleep in this state –
and truly asleep – to the things of the world and to
ourselves. As a matter of fact, during the time that the
union lasts the soul is left as though without its senses,
for it has no power to think even if it wants to. In loving,

if it does love, it doesn't understand how or what it is it loves or what it would want. In sum, it is like one who in every respect has died to the world so as to live more completely in God.

Teresa of Avila, *The Interior Castle*,
pt 5, ch. 1, para. 4, p. 336

Concluding prayers

SUNDAY

Introductory prayer

Psalm 150
Alleluia!

Praise God in his holy place,
praise him in the heavenly vault of his power,
praise him for his mighty deeds,
praise him for all his greatness.

Praise him with fanfare of trumpet,
praise him with harp and lyre,
praise him with tambourines and dancing,
praise him with strings and pipes,
praise him with the clamour of cymbals,
praise him with triumphant cymbals,
Let everything that breathes praise Yahweh.

Alleluia!

Gospel reading: Luke 24.13-17, 28-35
Now that very same day, two of them were on their
way to a village called Emmaus, seven miles from
Jerusalem, and they were talking together about all
that had happened. And it happened that as they
were talking together and discussing it, Jesus
himself came up and walked by their side; but their

eyes were prevented from recognising him. He said to them, 'What are all these things that you are discussing as you walk along?' They stopped, their faces downcast. . . .

When they drew near to the village to which they were going, he made as if to go on; but they pressed him to stay with him saying, 'It is nearly evening, and the day is almost over.' So he went in to stay with them. Now while he was with them at table, he took the bread and said the blessing; then he broke it and handed it to them. And their eyes were opened and they recognised him; but he had vanished from their sight. Then they said to each other, 'Did not our hearts burn within us as he talked to us on the road and explained the scriptures to us?'

They set out that instant and returned to Jerusalem. There they found the Eleven assembled together with their companions, who said to them, 'The Lord has indeed risen and has appeared to Simon.' Then they told their story of what had happened on the road and how they had recognised him at the breaking of bread.

Reading from the Church's tradition

It is good to find more solitude so as to make room for the Lord and allow His Majesty to work as though with something belonging to Him. At most, a gentle word from time to time is sufficient, as in the case of one who blows on a candle to enkindle it again when it begins to die out. But if the candle is burning, blowing on it will in my opinion serve no other purpose than to put it out. I say that the blowing should be gentle lest the will be distracted by the intellect busying itself with many words.

Teresa of Avila, *The Way of Perfection*,
ch. 31, para. 7, p. 156

Concluding prayers

Sources and Acknowledgements

The publisher and author acknowledge with thanks permission to reproduce extracts from the following. Every effort has been made to seek permission to use copyright material reproduced in this book. The publisher apologizes for those cases where permission might not have been sought and, if notified, will formally seek permission at the earliest opportunity.

Scripture quotations are taken from The New Jerusalem Bible, published and copyright © 1985 by Darton, Longman & Todd Ltd and Doubleday & Co., Inc., a division of Random House, Inc. and used by permission of Darton, Longman and Todd.

ICS Publications

Edith Stein, *Essays on Woman*, in *The Collected Works of Edith Stein*, II, trans. by Freda Mary Oben (Washington, DC: ICS Publications, 1996). From *Essays on Woman* by Edith Stein translated by Freda Mary Oben, Ph.D. Copyright © 1987, 1996 Washington Province of Discalced Carmelites ICS Publications 2131 Lincoln Road, N.E. Washington, DC 20002-1199 U.S.A. www.icspublications.org

Edith Stein, *The Hidden Life*, in *The Collected Works of Edith Stein*, IV (Washington, DC: ICS Publications, 1992). From *The Hidden Life* by Edith Stein Copyright © 1992 Washington Province of Discalced Carmelites ICS Publications 2131 Lincoln Road, N.E. Washington, DC 20002-1199 U.S.A. www.icspublications.org

Elizabeth of the Trinity, *Letters from Carmel*, in *The Complete Works of Elizabeth of the Trinity*, II (Washington, DC: ICS Publica-

121

tions, 1995), Letter 129. From *The Complete Works of Elizabeth of the Trinity, Volume Two* translated by Anne Englund Nash Copyright © 1995 by Washington Province of Discalced Carmelites ICS Publications 2131 Lincoln Road, N.E. Washington, DC 20002-1199 U.S.A. www.icspublications.org

John of the Cross, *The Ascent of Mount Carmel*, in *The Collected Works of Saint John of the Cross*, trans. by Kieran Kavanaugh and Otilio Rodriguez (Washington, DC: ICS Publications, 1991). From *The Collected Works of St. John of the Cross*, translated by Kieran Kavanaugh and Otilio Rodriguez Copyright © 1964, 1979, 1991 by Washington Province of Discalced Carmelites ICS Publications 2131 Lincoln Road, N.E. Washington, DC 20002-1199 U.S.A. www.icspublications.org

John of the Cross, 'The dark night', in *The Collected Works of Saint John of the Cross*, trans. by Kieran Kavanaugh and Otilio Rodriguez (Washington, DC: ICS Publications, 1991)

John of the Cross, *The Letters*, in *The Collected Works of Saint John of the Cross*, trans. by Kieran Kavanaugh and Otilio Rodriguez (Washington, DC: ICS Publications, 1991), letter 11

John of the Cross, *The Sayings of Light and Love*, in *The Collected Works of Saint John of the Cross*, trans. by Kieran Kavanaugh and Otilio Rodriguez (Washington, DC: ICS Publications, 1991)

John of the Cross, 'Song of the soul that rejoices in knowing God through faith', in *The Collected Works of Saint John of the Cross*, trans. by Kieran Kavanaugh and Otilio Rodriguez (Washington, DC: ICS Publications, 1991)

John of the Cross, 'The spiritual canticle', in *The Collected Works of Saint John of the Cross*, trans. by Kieran Kavanaugh and Otilio Rodriguez (Washington, DC: ICS Publications, 1991)

John of the Cross, *The Spiritual Canticle*, in *The Collected Works of Saint John of the Cross*, trans. by Kieran Kavanaugh and Otilio Rodriguez (Washington, DC: ICS Publications, 1991)

Teresa of Avila, *The Interior Castle*, in *The Collected Works of St. Teresa of Avila*, II, trans. by Kieran Kavanaugh and Otilio Rodriguez (Washington, DC: ICS Publications, 1980). From *The Collected Works of St. Teresa of Avila, Volume Two* translated by Kieran Kavanaugh and Otilio Rodriguez Copyright © 1980 by Washington Province of Discalced Carmelites ICS Publications 2131 Lincoln Road, N.E. Washington, DC 20002-1199 U.S.A. www.icspublications.org

Teresa of Avila, *Spiritual Testimonies*, in *The Collected Works of St. Teresa of Avila*, I, trans. by Kieran Kavanaugh and Otilio Rodriguez (Washington, DC: ICS Publications, 1987). From *The Collected Works of St. Teresa of Avila, Volume One*, translated by Kieran Kavanaugh and Otilio Rodriguez Copyright © 1976 by Washington Province of Discalced Carmelites ICS Publications 2131 Lincoln Road, N.E. Washington, DC 20002-1199 U.S.A. www.icspublications.org

Teresa of Avila, *The Way of Perfection*, in *The Collected Works of St. Teresa of Avila*, II, trans. by Kieran Kavanaugh and Otilio Rodriguez (Washington, DC: ICS Publications, 1980)

Thérèse of Lisieux, 'Act of oblation to Merciful Love', in *Story of a Soul: The Autobiography of Saint Thérèse of Lisieux*, trans. by John Clarke (Washington, DC: ICS Publications, 1996). From *Story of a Soul*, translated by John Clarke, O.C.D. Copyright © 1975, 1976, 1996 by Washington Province of Discalced Carmelites ICS Publications 2131 Lincoln Road, N.E. Washington, DC 20002-1199 U.S.A. www.icspublications.org

Thérèse of Lisieux, *Story of a Soul: The Autobiography of Saint Thérèse of Lisieux*, trans. by John Clarke (Washington, DC: ICS Publications, 1996)

Other copyright holders
Gerard W. Hughes, *God of Compassion* (London: CAFOD/Hodder & Stoughton, 1998). Permission sought from Hodder & Stoughton. Reproduced by permission of Gerard W. Hughes

Further Reading

If this collection of readings has inspired you to explore further, you may want to pray with the Church's Divine Office. This is the official prayer of the Church, so you will be uniting yourself in prayer with the whole Church while you do so. That is a comforting and strengthening thought! I would suggest either of the following:

Morning and Evening Prayer with Night Prayer from The Divine Office (London: Collins, 1976)

A Shorter Morning and Evening Prayer: The Psalter of The Divine Office with Selected Texts for the Seasons, Feasts of the Lord and Solemnities (London: Collins, 1983)

The first of these is the larger volume, with the full texts for the different seasons of the Church's year, and comes in a black cover. The second is incomplete but for that reason easier to follow, and is bound in red.

Introductory and Concluding Prayers

Introductory prayer

Verse: O God, come to our aid.

Response: O Lord, make haste to help us.

Remain in silence for a few minutes, pondering on the day and offering it to God

Lord, I offer myself to you this evening, placing all the events of the day before you, good and bad, easy and difficult. Help me to place everything in your arms, at the foot of your cross. Amen.

Concluding prayers

After the reading from the Church's tradition, take a moment to pray silently for your own and others' needs, and to just be in God's presence

Nunc Dimittis
Antiphon: Save us, Lord, while we are awake; protect us while we sleep; that we may keep watch with Christ and rest with him in peace.

At last, all-powerful Master,
you give leave to your servant
to go in peace, according to your promise.
For my eyes have seen your salvation
Which you have prepared for all nations,
the light to enlighten the Gentiles
and give glory to Israel, your people.
Repeat antiphon

Lord, as I prepare myself for sleep, come to me and
watch over me this night and every night. Keep me safe
until morning, when I shall rise ready to face the new
day. Amen.

Blessing
The Lord grant us a quiet night and a perfect end.
Response: Amen.

Salve Regina
Hail, holy Queen, mother of mercy,
our life, our sweetness, and our hope.
To you do we cry,
poor, banished children of Eve.
To you do we send up our sighs,
mourning and weeping in this valley of tears.
Turn then, most gracious advocate,
your eyes of mercy toward use,
and after this exile
show unto us the blessed fruit of your womb, Jesus.

O clement, O loving, O sweet Virgin Mary.

Salve, Regina, Mater misericordiae;
vita, dulcedo, et spes nostra, salve.
Ad te clamamus, exsules filii Hevae,
ad te suspiramus, gementes et flentes
in hac lacrimarum valle.
Eia, ergo, advocata nostra, illos tuos
misericordes oculos ad nos converte;
et Iesum, benedictum fructum ventris tui,
nobis post hoc exilium ostende.
O clemens, O pia, O dulcis Virgo Maria.